The Artistry of
Marian McPartland

ISBN: 0-89898-415-7

© 1985 Columbia Pictures Publications,
15800 N .W. 48th Avenue, Miami, Florida 33014
Transcriptions: Don Sickler and John Oddo
Production Coordinator: David C. Olsen

Introduction

Here are some of my favorite "standard" tunes. Transcribing my recorded improvisations in print shows real dedication and expertise by John Oddo and Don Sickler. It's not easy to write down music that is almost totally improvised. These were my thoughts of the moment, but they might change slightly next time I play the tune. It's like putting your feelings down on paper. The markings in **Laura,** for instance, are meant to indicate the ebb and flow of the melody (at least the way I think of it), and nuances come with knowing the lyrics. **Laura** is a tender, romantic tune, and it is harmonically attractive even without using alternate chord changes.

I suppose, in the classical sense, these transcriptions might not be considered altogether "correct," since they are actual improvisations, but the idea is to give you, the player, as much freedom as possible, within the scope of the written notes and the harmonic structure.

There is no strict ruling as to how any of these have to be played. The markings are more of a guide than anything else, and the tempos can be varied according to your own conception. On all of them try to listen to yourself. And don't over pedal!! In a sense, the sustaining pedal is like having your foot on the gas pedal in a car. You press it by instinct: at times a gentle touch, sometimes a heavier pressure. If you practice with just your left hand alone, you can feel how much pedal to use — but never let the notes sound "blurry." Hear the right hand lines in your head, or you can sing them to yourself.

If you know the lyrics to the songs, you can play off them in a sensitive way. **For All We Know** is in the key of A, because to me that key sets up such good vibrations, being a very "alive" key. Sometimes a melody seems to dictate what the key should be (at least it does for me), so that it can be played in a certain register of the piano. I like the middle range for starting the melody in the beginning to set up the tune.

When the bass player on the record is playing the roots, as in **Sweet and Lovely** and **Close Your Eyes,** you should be able to hear them in your head — even though they aren't shown in this transcription.

Emily has a rubato feeling going into a lightly swinging tempo, but you can experiment with it, letting it rise and fall, never letting it be too stiff. Use a metronome. Practice each hand separately. You can use a metronome as the "rhythm section" and also to check the steadiness of your time feelings. (Lennie Tristano advised me to do this years ago, and I still do it. That was good advice.)

Above all, you are meant to have fun with these pieces. Experiment with your own ideas, phrasing, and choice of voicings. Jazz being the personal form of expression that it is, you can put your own imprint on each piece. You should, if possible, check the sheet music to learn these songs. They are all available (the publishers are cited with each composition) and you can get an idea of what the original chords and melodies are like before you take off and do your own thing. Good luck to you!

Marian McPartland.

"Marian McPartland ...A Reflection"
by J. Tevere McFadyen

On a cluttered side table in her Manhattan apartment, Marian McPartland keeps a remarkable photograph. The picture was taken on a summer morning some twenty-five years ago. It shows the front steps and stoop of a Harlem brownstone brimming with jazz notables — an historic musicians' class portrait overflowing onto the street. Here is Count Basie, grinning, squatting on the curb amidst a gabble of local urchins. Here is Gerry Mulligan seeming almost adolescent, clowning for the camera with an ageless Dizzy Gillespie. Dizzy's tongue is extended — "Naturally," Marian says — toward the camera. Here's Charles Mingus looking young and robust. Here's Thelonious Monk in a rakish hat and dark glasses. Here is Bud Freeman and Max Kamisky, Buster Bailey and Philly Joe Jones, Red Allen, Oscar Pettiford, and a saxophone giants Coleman Hawkins and Lester Young. Here too is Marian McPartland, standing at ease in the middle foreground, chatting with a svelte and lovely Mary Lou Williams. Marian wears a sleeveless summer gown that drapes smoothly over her trim frame. She looks utterly comfortable and radiates effortless poise. Her head is thrown back—naturally—in a laugh.

As a working jazz musician, Marian McPartland is laughing still. She is busier now than she's ever been—a white British woman who has carved out a secure place for herself in a progession long dominated by black American men. Marian seems unable to operate at less than full throttle. She tours tirelessly, often accompanied by bassist Gary Mazzaroppi, playing every place; festivals and clubs to classrooms and concert halls. She owns her own record company — Halcyon Records — yet takes time to record a steady stream of albums on the Concord Jazz label as well. For her radio program, "Marian McPartland's Piano Jazz" on National Public Radio, she interviews and accompanies well-known guests whose pianistic proclivities run from sedate swing to agreesive avant garde. The Peabody-Award-winning show started its seventh consecutive year on the air in October of 1985. McPartland is also an active composer (her "Twilight World," with words by lyricist Johnny Mercer, has become something of a standard since it was recorded by Tony Bennett). Lately she has begun to have her taped improvisations transcribed, with an eye toward creating an extended work for piano and orchestra. She acknowledges laughing, "I'd really kind of like to write a song Frank Sinatra would sing." Marian McParland likes to do many things, but what she likes to do best is play. "I guess that's really still my greatest kick," she allows. "Just sitting around and playing."

Margaret Marian Turner was born in Slough, near Windsor, Buckinghamshire. The daughter of upper middle class parents, she first approached a piano—her uncle's—at age three. She subsequently put in several years showing off for family gatherings, and at nine was leveraged into a doomed attempt at the violin. She went off to boarding school, then wound up at London Guildhall School of Music, where she studied piano and composition. "I wrote some things then which, to my astonishment, still stand up pretty well," she remarks. "I've been trying to relearn them, but I'm such a miserable reader that it puts me off." She knuckled down long enough to come under the lasting spell of Ravel and Debussy, and especially Delius, but her commitment flagged. "My God, was I fortunate!" she recalls. "I had a boyfriend who loved jazz and brought all his records over to the house. We'd sit for hours listening to Benny Goodman and Duke Ellington, Bud Freeman, Mugsy Spannier, and all the piano players: Art Tatum, Fats Waller, James P. Johnson, you name it." Marian abandoned the Guildhall at twenty to join a four-piano vaudeville act.

Back in 1943, Marian signed on to do USO camp shows in Belgium and France, where she met and fell "madly in love" with Chicago cornetist and Bix Beiderbecke protege, Jimmy McPartland, whose name she soon added to hers. They played at their own wedding. The two later divorced, but as she puts it, "The divorce didn't work, or maybe it did," and today they're happily unmarried while sharing adjacent halves of a Long Island duplex. Marian credits Jimmy with providing much of the impetus and support for her assault on the male bastions of jazz, and for helping to shape her early playing as well. Though they diverged musically when she began exploring more abstract contemporary ideas, feeling her way toward her own lyrical and modern melodic balance, the two still perform together whenever they get the chance. Marian's musical debt to Jimmy may quirkily surface in a rollicking "Royal Garden Blues," or in a snatch of potent left hand bass spliced into "I'm Old Fashioned."

If Jimmy held the door initially, making it possible, for instance, for Marian to inaugurate her trio career at New York's prestigious Embers Club backed by two top sidemen, she rapidly established her own credentials. For eight years beginning in 1952 she settle into the Hickory House, becoming in the process a consummate club pianist. This is a talent too often taken for granted. The top-flight club player has to cover the classics without falling prey to lurking cliches. Her repertoire must be for all practical purposes infinite and her tolerance of less than ideal conditions eternal. The performer's stamp of individuality may under no circumstances obscure a song's familiar origins, yet the ability to play the same material night after night relies heavily on constant inventiveness. The finest cafe performers—and Marian McPartland is surely one—labor brilliantly in the line of fire. Anyone tempted to pass this capacity off as minor would do well to wonder how Vladimir Horowitz might react if plunked down at two in the morning in a smoky room full of clinking glasses, mindless conversations, and loudly hissed requests for "Satin Doll" and "Misty."

As McPartland's interests and ambitions expanded, she discovered that she was no longer content to pursue the linear path toward nightclub success. Increasingly caught up in composition and growing slowly more self-assured, she began tentatively to offer her own tunes mixed into sets of standards. She found unexpected inspiration in contemporary tunes and allowed herself to renovate old favorites, inventing new interpretations often branded by her bubbling spring of humor. For

what has become one of her signature pieces, she tossed three distinctly different eras together in an unlikely melange: Jerome Kern's "Yesterdays" entwines easily with Paul McCartney's "Yesterday," and the two detour fluidly for a long stretch in the middle into a Bach-like contrapuntal fugue.

Her still-evolving style is confidently eclectic. She touches on every era of jazz, skipping lightly from Fats Waller to Duke Ellington to John Coltrane. She plays showtunes, often in surprising renditions with revised tempi. She demonstrates an obvious affection for what Alec Wilder dubbed "American popular song," and she unrepentantly includes Stevie Wonder's or Billy Joel's compositions in her club sets.

McPartland rarely resorts to flamboyance or pyrotechnics. Her touch is delicate. Her primary tools are texture and dynamics. Her tunes are three dimensional. Her arrangements resemble drawings made from countless seemingly random pen and ink hatchmarks: images slowly coalescing into something startlingly simple and powerful. She edits as she plays following spontaneous notes to unanticipated distinations, then returning without remorse to restate a previous phrase, slightly altered. She decorates incessantly, and in fact, has had to train herself to leave spaces where the air can blow through. "I'm trying," she says, "to play fewer notes."

The result of these efforts is a peculiarly elusive style, one which evades easy categorization. McPartland is a modern player, in that she neither composes nor performs within the confines of any historic genre, yet she has nothing in common with the experimental fringe. She is a gracious and flexible pianist who, in the estimation of **New Yorker** magazine jazz critic Whitney Balliett, has "moved beyond adroit adulation into her own, special realm. It is, in the way of Johnny Hodges and Sidney Bechet and Tatum, an emotional, romantic, and highly inventive one."

Marian McPartland plays fewer club dates nowadays ("I can't stand the noise anymore"), but more concerts. To make room for orchestrations of her own tunes ("Twilight World" and "In The Days of Our Love") and eventually—hopefully—for her major work-in-progress, "Silent Spring," a suite for piano and orchestra built around environmental themes. She professes to be happy with her work to date, but anxious, as ever, to explore new realms. "I really do feel as if I'm still learning," she reflects. "Of course, there are times when I think I play badly, but there are other times—a few at least—when I actually think I'm getting better."

"I'm glad I'm not a singer or dancer," she muses, "because then I'd probably have to quit sooner or later. In this business I can go on forever." She gives every indication of intending to do just that. She looks and acts at least twenty years younger than she is, and she watches her health. She keeps a Red Cross Pacard on her piano that reads: THANK YOU FOR NOT SMOKING. She knocks on wood. She skirts wide round intimations of retirement—"I really think musicians ought to be exempt from that, don't you?"—and admits that she just can't imagine leaving the thick of things. "I do love it," she says, "and there's so much I haven't done yet. I can't stop now. I wouldn't dare. It's a race, you know, and I can't afford to lose my place." She gleams. "Besides," she adds, smiling, "I enjoy it. It doesn't feel much like work to me."

And it doesn't sound much like work either.

EMILY

**Words by
JOHNNY MERCER**

**Music by
JOHNNY MANDEL**

Emily - 9 - 1

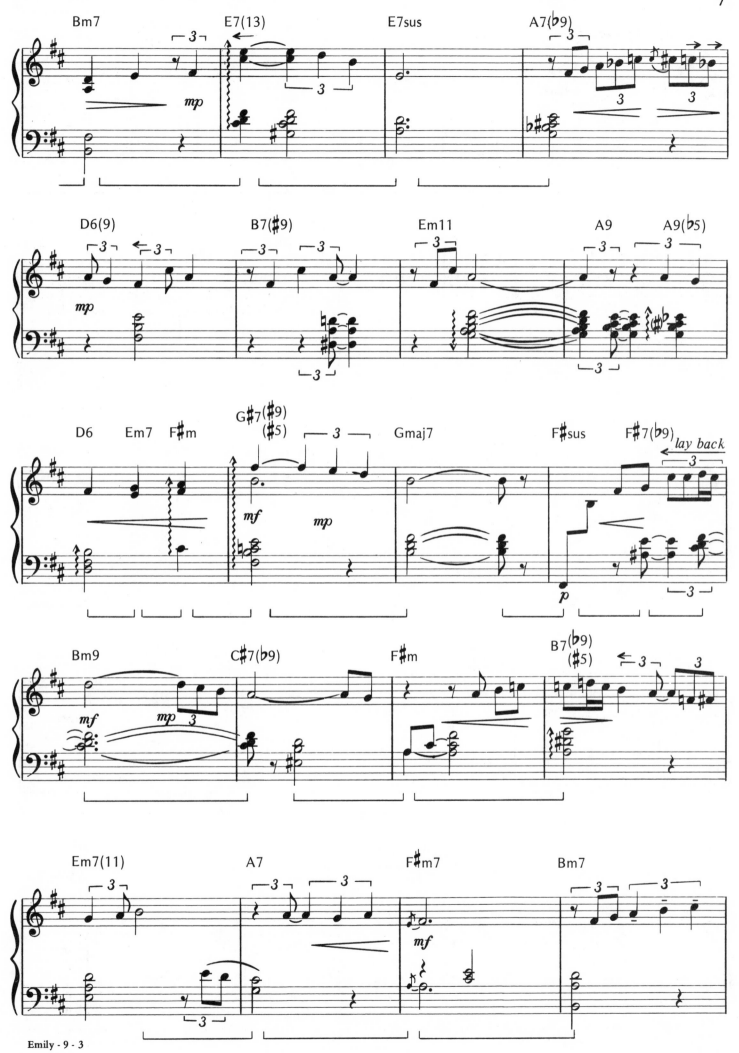

Emily - 9 - 3

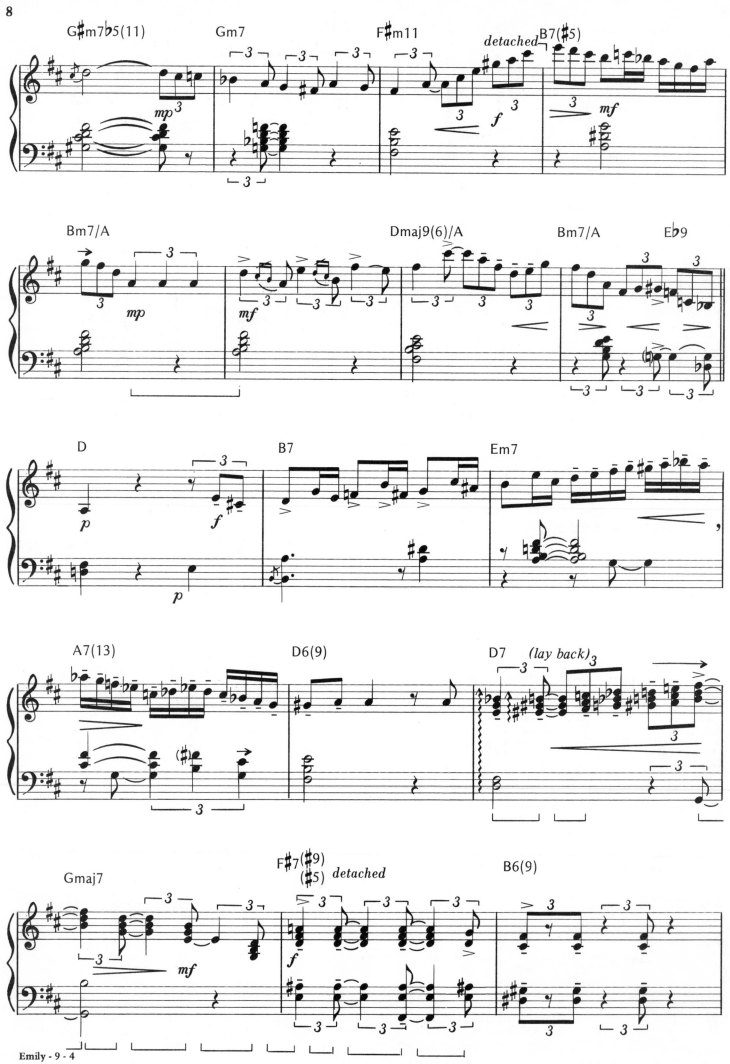

a touch of pedal - - - - - - - - - - ┘

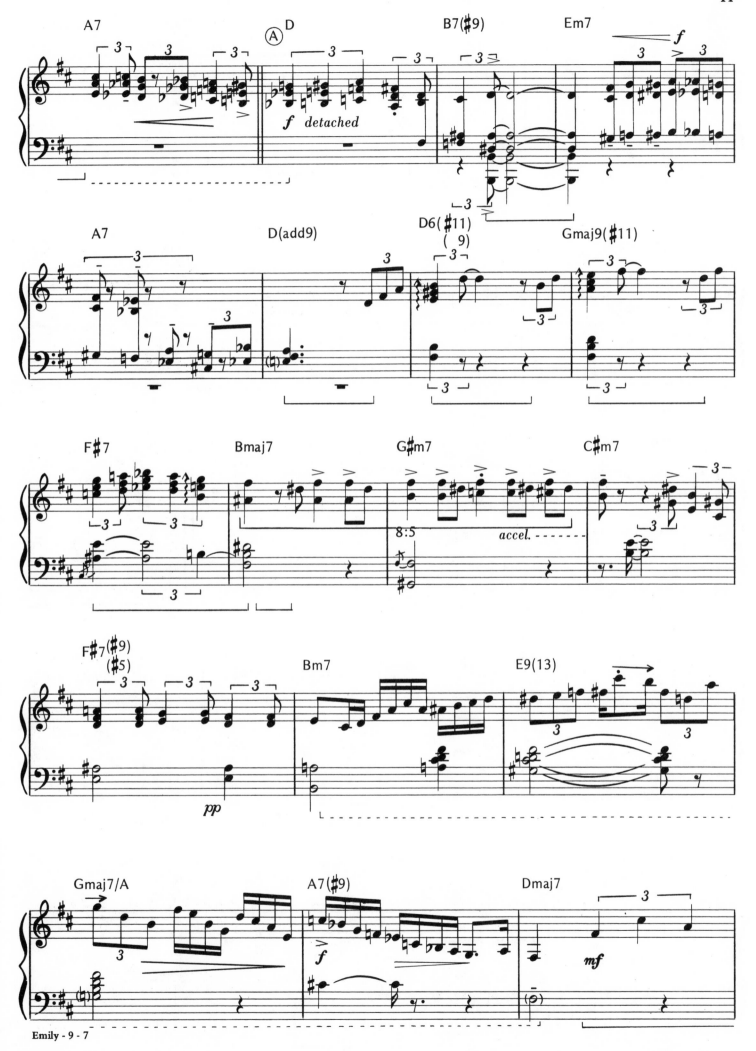

12

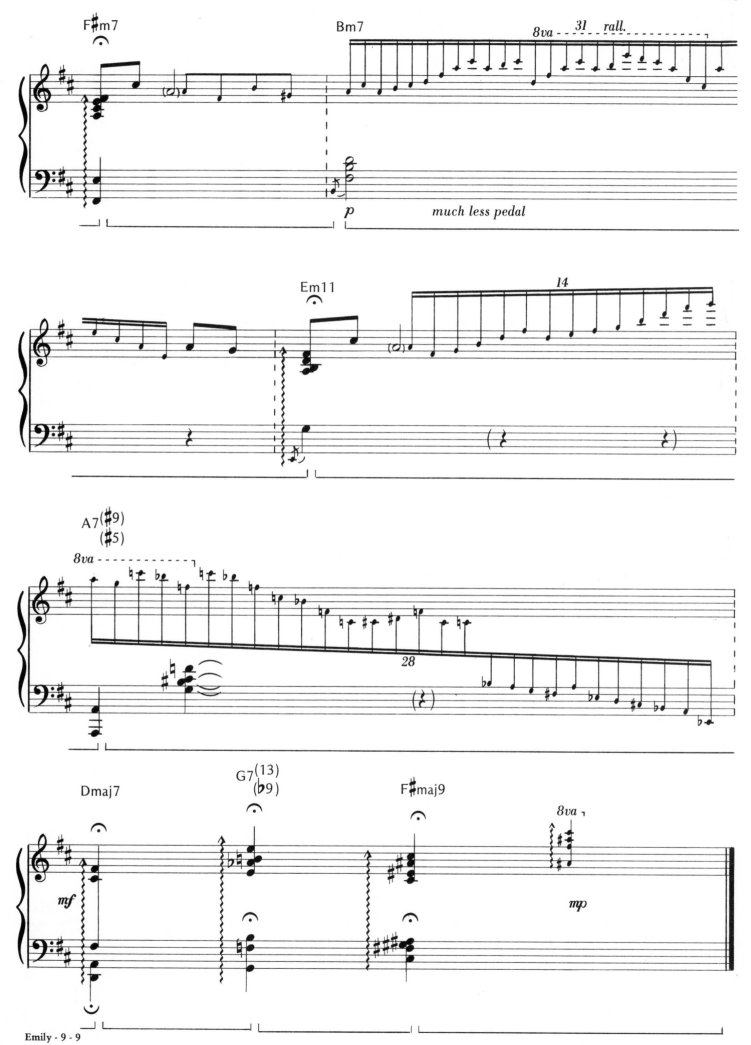

SWEET AND LOVELY

Words and Music by
GUS ARNHEIM, HARRY TOBIAS
and JULES LEMARE

Bass and drums start with 4 measures to set up the feeling.

Sweet And Lovely - 10 - 1

Sweet And Lovely - 10 - 2

Sweet And Lovely - 10 - 6

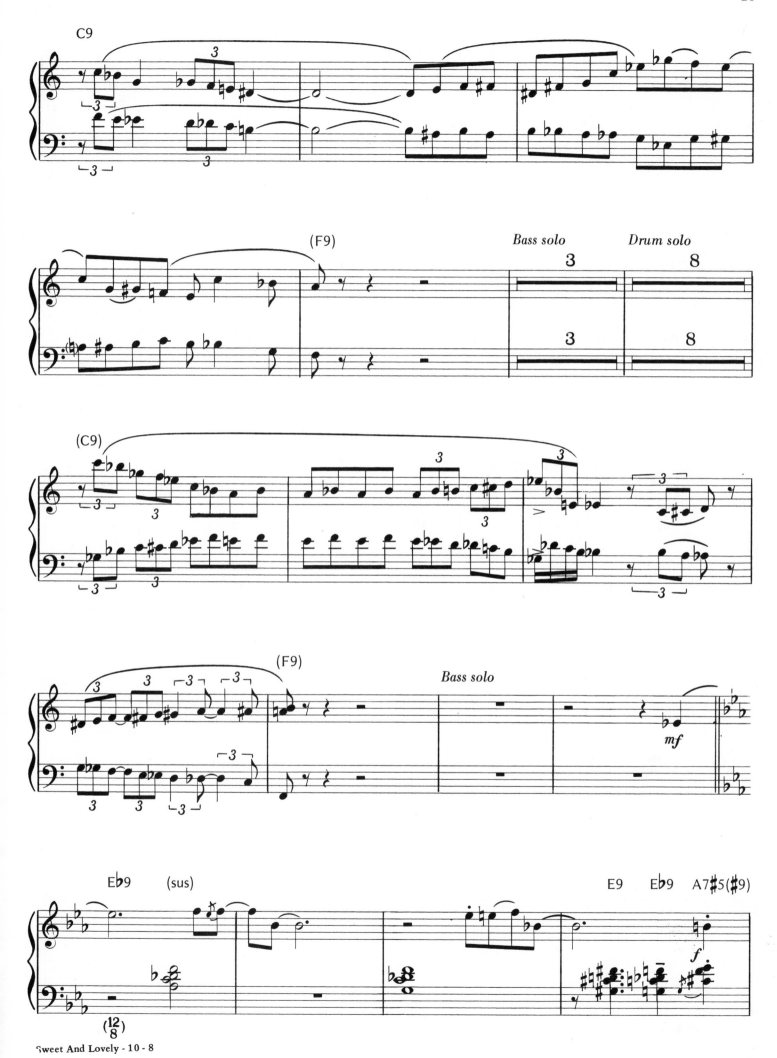

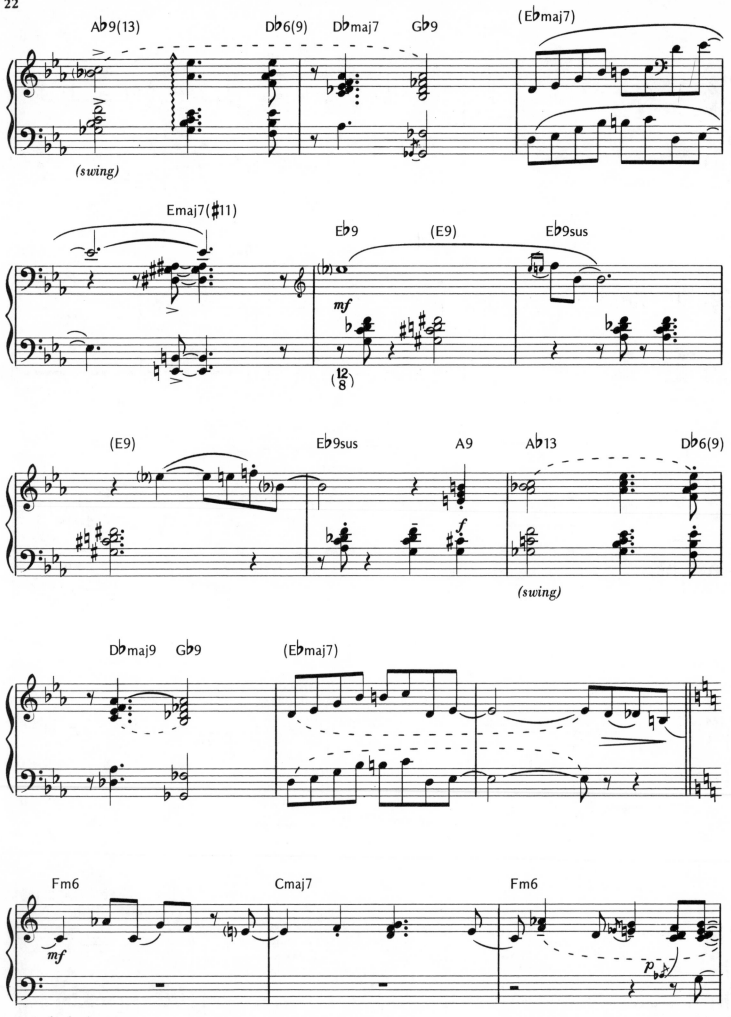

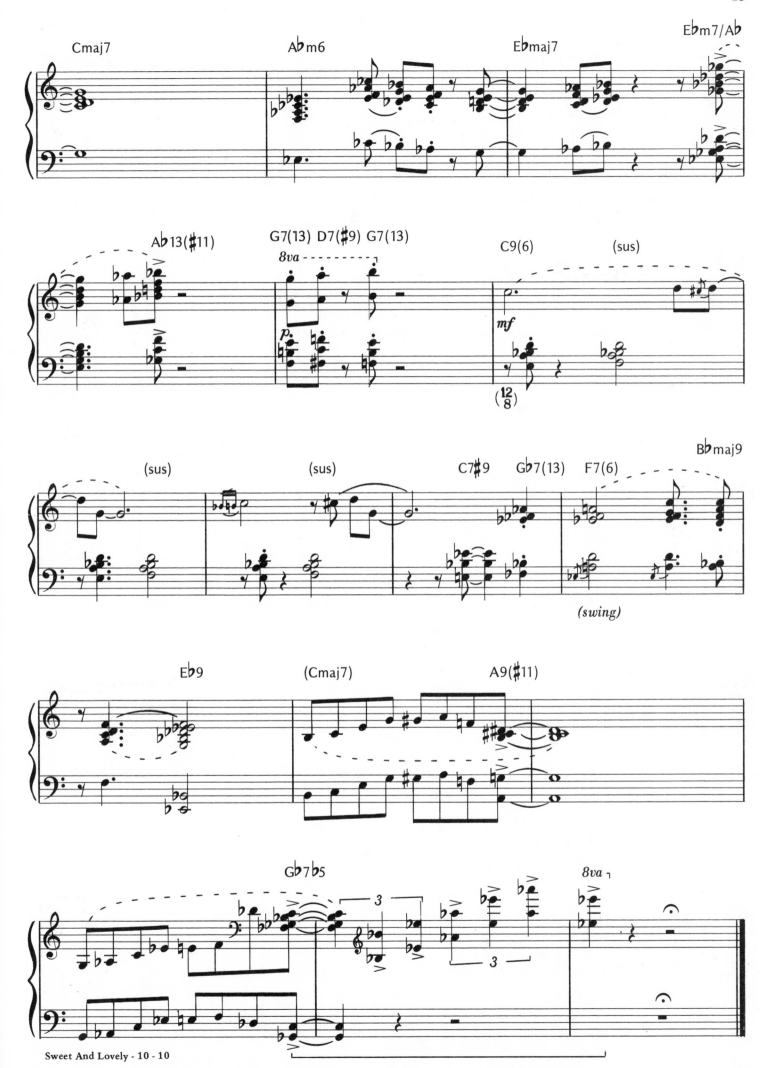

LAURA

Words by
JOHNNY MERCER

Music by
DAVID RASKIN

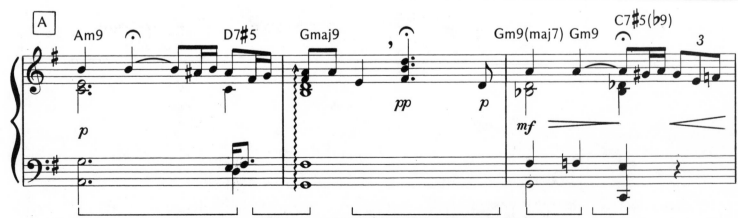

Laura - 6 - 1

Jazz waltz feeling

Laura - 6 - 2

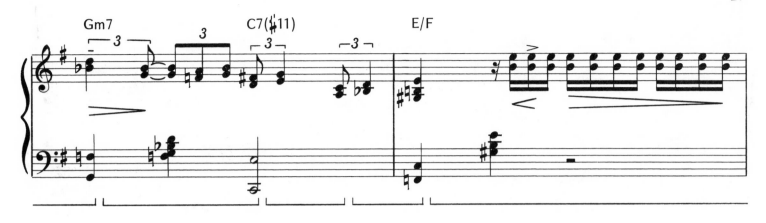

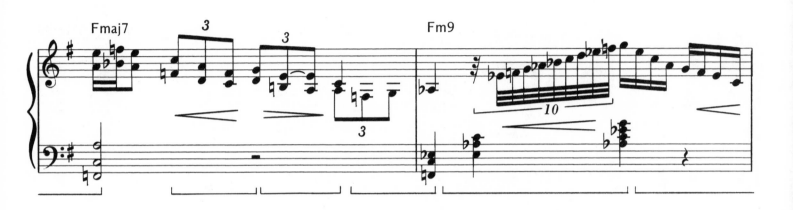

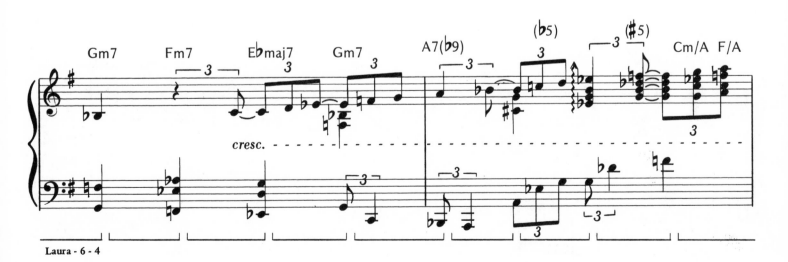

Laura - 6 - 4

Laura - 6 - 6

CLOSE YOUR EYES

Words and Music by
BERNICE PETKERE

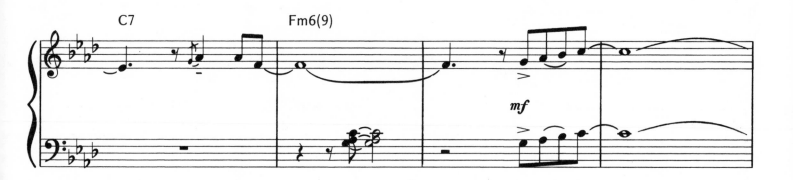

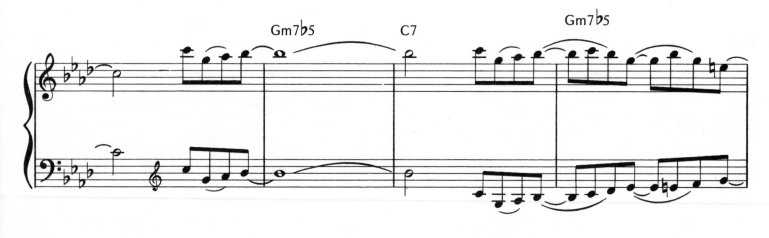

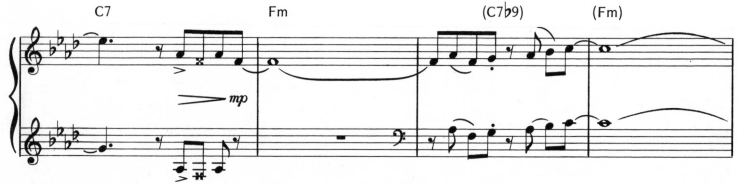

Close Your Eyes - 15 - 1

Close Your Eyes - 15 - 2

32

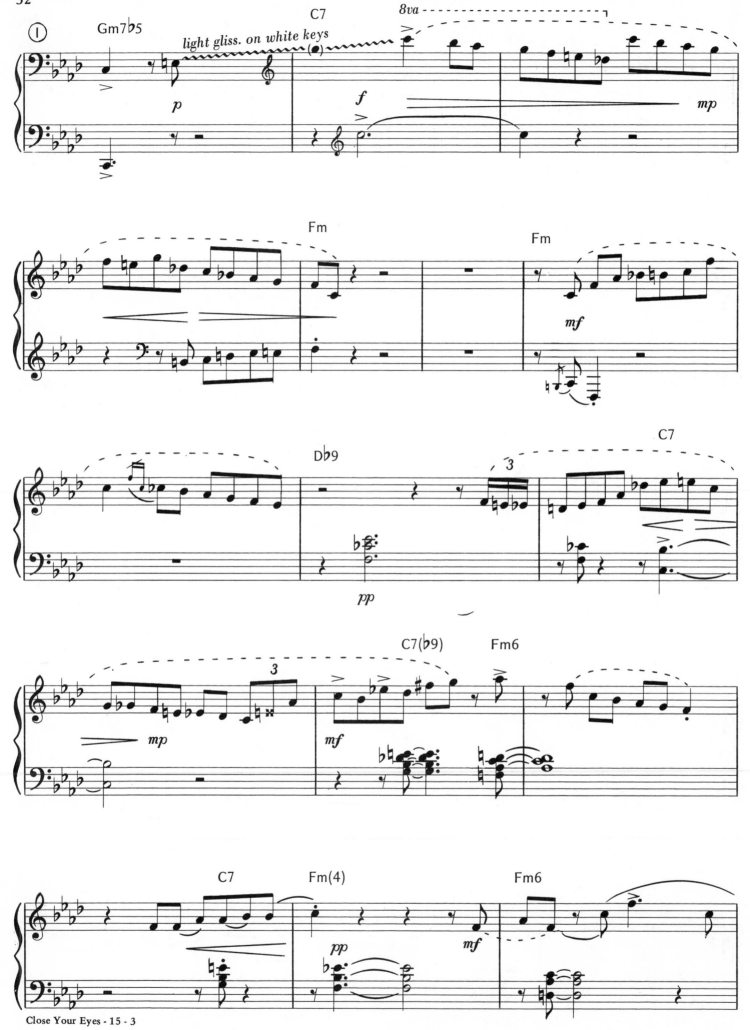

Close Your Eyes - 15 - 4

Close Your Eyes - 15 - 6

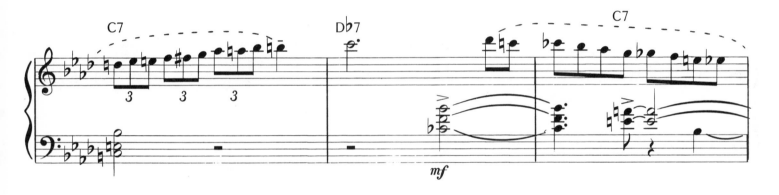

42

Close Your Eyes - 15 - 13

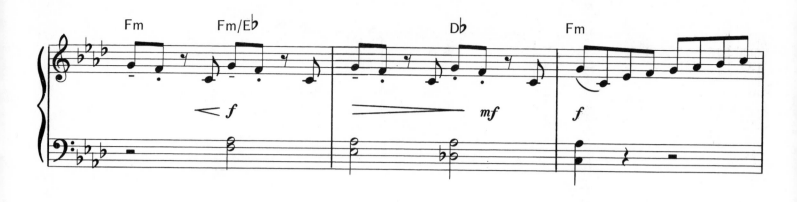

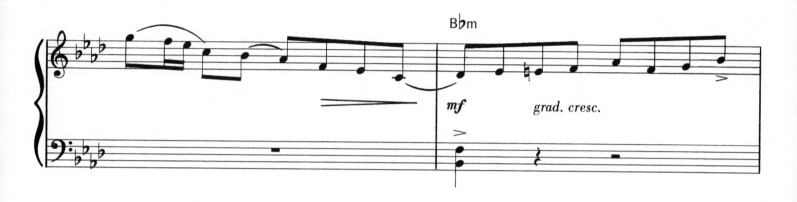

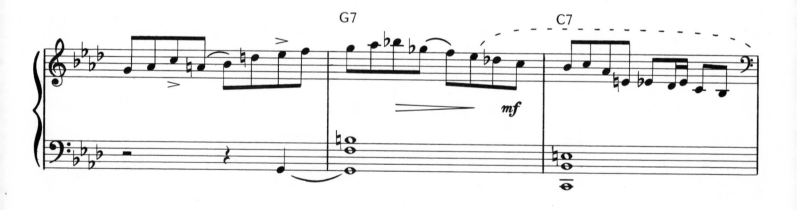

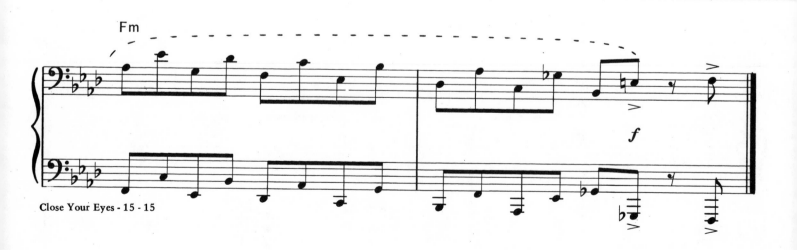

IF YOU COULD SEE ME NOW

Lyric by
CARL SIGMAN

Music by
TAD DAMERON

If You Could See Me Now - 5 - 1

If You Could See Me Now - 5 - 3

Halcyon No. 117 LIVE AT THE CARLYLE Side 2 Track 4

FOR ALL WE KNOW

Words by
SAM M. LEWIS

Music by
J. FRED COOTS

For All We Know - 6 - 1

For All We Know - 6 - 2

For All We Know - 6 - 4

For All We Know - 6 - 6

CPP/Belwin, Inc.
15800 N.W. 48th Avenue
Miami, FL 33014

ISBN: 0-89898-415-7

TPF0135

A
PUBLICATION